Brittle Bones

JANET FISHER was born in Birmingham in 1943. She read Law at Bristol University, followed by five years' legal publishing experience. After a move to Yorkshire and a period of illness, she began to develop herself as a writer. In 1989 she joined The Poetry Business in Huddersfield as co-director with Peter Sansom. She has had two previous main poetry collections: *Listening to Dancing* (1996) and *Women Who Dye Their Hair* (2001).

Also by Janet Fisher

Women Who Dye Their Hair (Smith/Doorstop, 2001)
Listening to Dancing (Smith/Doorstop, 1996)

Brittle Bones

Janet Fisher

CAMBRIDGE

PUBLISHED BY SALT PUBLISHING
PO Box 937, Great Wilbraham, Cambridge CB21 5JX United Kingdom

First published 2008

Printed and bound in the United Kingdom by Biddles Ltd, King's Lynn, Norfolk

Typeset in Swift 9.5 / 13

ISBN 978 1 84471 402 5 hardback

Salt Publishing Ltd gratefully acknowledges
the financial assistance of Arts Council England

1 3 5 7 9 8 6 4 2

For Ray, with love

Contents

Acknowledgements

Thanks are due to the editors of the following, where versions of some of these poems first appeared: *Guardian Unlimited, Interpreter's House, Magma, Mslexia, PN Review, Richmond Review, Smiths Knoll, Stride, The Wide Skirt.*

'Chopsticks' won first prize in the Pitshanger Poets Competition 2006.

There are many people (you know who you are) to thank for their advice and encouragement, but I give special thanks to Peter Sansom for his wise editing and friendship over twenty years.

Getting There

It was a long way off

and she had no map

or compass   nothing

but the lie of the land

under her boots

and the stars in her head.

Chopsticks

('Room in New York': Edward Hopper)

He pretends to read the paper and I
fiddle with the keyboard. We don't bother
to draw the blinds. There's nothing to see.
Some nights when it's hot I take an axe
to that dumb head with its parting just so, the way
it catches the light, and some nights I just sit.

I once had a yen to learn piano so they sent me
to Miss Silver whose cottage stank
and she taught me the scale of C: 1, 2, 3 thumb under,
but we had no instrument at home
and I never got as far as the black notes

but whenever I hear a Chopin mazurka,
or a café pianist vamps Cole Porter,
I dream over what I've not done, like
digging for rocks in China or learning to fly.
The sky's so blue above the clouds.

Once in the street I heard a man shout
'There are no oranges in Nevada'
and it made me want to go there.

Rusholme

Someone died in this room
and someone didn't die,
heart beating like a boy on a trampoline,
or fall into a coma staring
at the porcelain shepherdess
poised, hand cupped to one ear
listening to distant music.
Someone who sat on the bed with an empty glass,
reaching out to straighten the rug.

Our Lady

You might, if you wanted, step from this window
onto the roof, walk across slates to other windows,
other rooms, or rest on the wooden chair

by the tub of camellias. The wind might be blowing leaves
across your stained boards, and always or sometimes
rain might shine on the panes and the distant trees.

She'll be out in the city somewhere
but she'll have left her scarf hanging on a hook.
A bird might pick from crumbs you'd thrown it

and beyond the houses the bells of Our Lady
might be summoning you into the clammy air.

Foster Place

You're in the hallway.
A door you haven't seen before
leads to a part you didn't know existed
or had forgotten: a new attic,
or steps leading to a terrace above a garden,
sunlight edging round the roof of the lean-to.
Turn back from the leaves, the sweet air, the distant cows,
and climb the stairs. There's a sofa tucked away.
Artists' folders, books, are piled at your elbow,
left a century ago when the reader popped out for a smoke.
A wooden chair, its grain like contours or ribbed sand,
a camel bag slung across a clothes horse,
a doll's house, toys, half hidden. A beech husk.
Hanging from the slant ceiling, a brass censer
sways though there's no breeze.
A fly's jagged buzz beats against the dormer.
In the wall is a small door.

Brittle Bones

birds' legs, dried stalks
a Chinese vase, a baby's wave
slivers of green on dead laburnum
tracks translucent up an arm
chalk line on a pavement, a child's logic
fingers pressing a wine glass stem
change of key on the downbeat
worn paths tracing the grass
a moon thumbprinted on a light sky
an old woman's face, her knuckles
strands of breath on a sharp morning
cracked glaze on a bedroom jug
its pattern of blue ivy and pouting lip
the roots I clutch at on the way up

For Ella

The is-not
of your not-yet-ness
like a wave
pulled back
into the sea
there and not there
your having-been-ness
                    drowns us

Mud

In my dream I find boots in the hall cupboard
flaking mud from our last holiday in North Wales
thirty years ago—the day they all went up Snowdon
and I stayed behind to look after the baby

who's now standing beside me in his old windcheater,
the one he wore on his houseboat, hands tight on the rail
against the wind, hair frizzy with rain. I smile
and he turns his head away but I see the tears

and dirt smears on his cheeks. His hands
have dirt on them too, and his nails are broken
as if he had been scratching deep into soil and stone
in search of a treasure he had unaccountably lost.

Hope

There's no accounting for Hope, the way it catches you
like an enemy from behind, its hairy fingers
gripping your shoulders, its knee in the small of your back.
You trip, you're bound to, no one could keep their balance
though all you want is to trudge on, head down, into the wind,
arms full of the heavy parcels you've been ordered to carry.

And how can you not surrender? The hands are in fact gentle,
they didn't mean to hurt, they're the hands of the teacher
who broke your clay castle, the one you were taking home
for Mother's Day, and her smiling apology bruises you:
you know you're supposed to be angry but how can you be? Strange.

The map Hope sketches for you with a wet finger in the dried mud
points the way you should be going but you're not ready and anyway
the map's wrong, but Hope's sad eyes pull you round
and guilt sharpens: how can you offend such a harmless creature?

Of the pains naughty Pandora released into the world,
this last little buzzing treasure causes you more trouble than
        anything—
gets in your way, spits in your eye, then just before leaving
shows you the future that might be instead of the one that is.

Turano

The way the trains pan out means two hours
in a border town — time to find a cash point
and lunch. This is Italy: peeling terracotta,
stucco saints chipped back to the concrete,
a door half open on a dark church.
Mary's heart is pierced with swords,
candles lit for her or those she prays for.
I have no change, my tears will do.

A restless waiter brings bulbous glasses
of the local wine; its bouquet
turns my head. You pick at bread
while we wait for risotto.
'Bread and wine', you say,
'what else do we need?'

Skellig Michael

Just the cold and the quiet
and gannets flying in long lines
from light to dark to light
across the face of the rocks
like angels seeking audience.

Sky set clear for the day,
a studded sea: you'd think
the monks hadn't a bad time of it.
Six centuries of storms and guilt—
there are many monuments to failure.

The world's mysterious enough,
laying down its legends like jewels.
Any wish could come true here.
They say walking on Skellig
can change your life. I'd best take care.

Narrow steps thin out, no handrails.
I have to imagine the beehive huts,
the high point to the east where they saw
—miracle or trick of the light—
the sun dancing on Easter morning.

The Wall

'Art — *a house that tries to be haunted*'
— EMILY DICKINSON

We're shivering. Draughts whisk
under carved doors, round pictures
framed in old wood of women talking.
The light won't catch us here.

I browse through the ancient bestiary
left just for us to look at. That's trust.
A dangerous animal bursts from its pages,
runs across the fields under the elm trees.

Next-door's down for the weekend
full of caesareans and melanoma. Peabirds step and point.
Even weeds have their place.

From the uneven bricks
in the barn wall
a web hangs loose.

At supper, after three bottles
we're onto nonsense about angels,
their haloes of Byzantine blue,
their emerald eyes.

Summer

Horsetail, buttercup,
rosebay willowherb,
hogweed, hawkweed,
foxglove, vetch,
rowan and raspberry,
blackberry, cow parsley,
hawthorn, blackthorn,
sycamore, birch.

~

Razzle dazzle, singed to a sizzle
in amongst the furze and thistle
breathe the heat haze, let it jostle
up your nose and round your tonsils;
dogs'll snooze and bumble bees'll
buzz and sun-bruised blooms will frazzle.

~

Wings of dancing insects glisten.
All things stretch and grow and ripen.

Cold Front

A promised frost, the first frost of November,
the way it stuns the air. The window
is a barrier to another room, the double

of this one, the same pictures on the wall.
Words are a static buzz. The best that can be said is
it doesn't exist but is there waiting

like the tick of a clock, an apple half eaten
in a blue bowl. Clouds settle like islands,
their shadows valleys for the moon to walk in.

Wishes

Midnight we lurch
across the Charles Bridge
lay our hands on the wishing stone.
Our wishes sink,
weighted bodies,
origins forgotten, fish food.

The Jew from Krakow,
driven by dreams, found his treasure
under his own hearthstone.
We've wandered the continent,
planned routes, crossed borders.
We rest where it's safest, out of the wind.

Let's drop a line over the parapet,
draw up waterweed
or a fish with a coin in its mouth.

Girl With Ferret

In a back street in Krakow behind the Great Square
where a trumpeter plays the fractured *hajnal* each hour
—six hundred years in honour of him who died
sounding the alarm, with an arrow in his throat—

the Museum opens once or twice a week
exhibiting a rare Leonardo: the ferret-faced girl
holding what may be a ferret, or an ermine,
from which one day someone will fashion a trim.

I'm told she was his patron's mistress, but
I believe she was a shy, slim-hipped boy
with long hair and a winsome smile
whom Leonardo found quivering in the corner

under some cloaks, clutching his only friend,
escaping the intentions of the strange men
who hung around his mother's apartment,
his throat sore with abuse and terror

and the artist scooped him up, pet and all,
into a place of safety, framing him.

Border Crossing
August 1991

We doze all the way from Belgium,
a bomber's moon over the Rhine.
At dawn lean men in greatcoats
apologise, check passports, as thirsty
for air we stumble from the hot bus
into the pine mists and the old stories.

We swap our cash for Crowns, count
Škodas commuting west. Fifty to the pound.
Our road leads beyond hostilities
to flowers on a pavement: 'obesit kommunistu',
candles for heroes, a young street singer
sheer as the crystal we buy in the Square.

'She Sips a Pale White Cup of Tea'

The mother in her usual lace stares through the window
as voices turn and fade in the dark passages between the mountains.
Slates gleam in offset sun, marbled birds cushion the thunder.

The lace punishes the arms of the mother, its tight whorls grip her veins,
her neck like the neck of a waterbird gleams like marble.
Voices gleam in her head. Cushioned she fades into slate.

Passages turn from the window.
Thunder springs softly across the mountains.
No one, least of all you, will ever know.

St Petersburg

The sun's a red dandelion over Palace Square.
A girl walks her harnessed ferret
past shivering squaddies rehearsing
for Victory Day. White faced men
push knocked off icons.

An hour's queuing in April wind
and I'm under the chandeliers
in the Winter Palace. Strings strike up,
a gleaming man in dress uniform
clicks, bows, takes my hand for the waltz.

A city of poets and bridges,
built on swamp. In Pushkin's house
I order hot chocolate, spiced apple.
Balloons bunch from the tram wires
like cheap red caviar.

The Dress

I covet brilliance, a lash
of silver wire
at the waist.

She lifts me
out of my box fresh
from the dressmaker's
fingers, a pinprick
of blood on the seam,
a perfect finish.

Now she's wearing me,
smoothing her hips.
That's what I do to her,
how good I make her feel.

I know she's dreaming
of wide floors, the dance,
and I am too, my skirt
trailing
a beat behind
as she spins in his arms.

It's silly to think
of a dress melting,
but that's what I dread:
a puddled heap abandoned
in the bedroom's heat.

Looking for the Chocolate Factory, Co. Kerry
11 September, 2001

A sunny start, a good forecast.
We trace the journey on the map.
The sky is white with September mist.
The Chocolate Factory's our next stop.

We trace the journey on the map.
The radio's on for the news headlines.
The Chocolate Factory's our next stop.
They're working hard to meet their deadlines.

The radio's on for the news headlines.
We stand and listen by the scales.
They're working hard to meet their deadlines,
They haven't got much left for sale.

We stand and listen by the scales.
All the girls are packing stock.
They haven't got much left for sale.
3,000 boxes for New York.

All the girls are packing stock,
Irish chocolate, sweet and rich.
3,000 boxes for New York.
The airplane's ready for dispatch.

Irish chocolate, sweet and rich.
A sunny start, a good forecast.
The airplane's ready for dispatch.
The sky's white with September mist.

What Shall We Do Now?

Drum up a cliché, act it bit by bit, dumb,
or cribbage: plastic pegs leapfrogging the holes—
one for his nob, two for his clean pair of heels.
Snap, Rummy, Go Fish, Sorry.
Or Scrabble, themed on sex or Election Day.
Monopoly: you have the top hat,
me the iron or the boot.
Or a bit of screen violence: Street Fighter, Doom,
scrambling up the levels with clues and code words.
Or the drip-turn-drop monotony
of blocks falling like bombs
between layers of skyscrapers
on a foggy Manhattan riverscape.

Get Over It

There are those who aren't good at things, who don't know, for example, how to use a mobile or give up smoking or read a map, and instead of feeling stupid they wear their ignorance as a badge of how much better they are as people. To hear them talk about their lack of achievement you'd think they were members of an exclusive club that would blackball them if they so much as hinted that they always check the oil or back up their hard disk, instead of being outcasts who won't get off their high horses and slum it with the rest of us who know how to do things without making a fuss.

To a Secret Agent

Pick a picture. They all look like you.
That one? Yes, I thought so.
Keep money on you at all times—sleep with it:
you'll need a guide across the territory.
Passwords are important but forgotten sometimes
if the other person doesn't trust you.
It's easy to spot your own kind
in a train or café (something about the eyes)
but not double agents:
they're too much inside their own skin.
Never draw attention to yourself.
Don't carry secrets in your shoes.
Think in their language. Never ask names.
Don't turn your head when yours is called.
Always buy a return ticket:
you want them to think you're coming back.
When the end's in sight, get there first.

Moving Pictures

The broad with the Marcel wave is perched on a bar stool, martini in hand, smiling at the joe in a stetson. He's out of town and green as the prairie. The pianist in the corner plays what passes for slow jazz, derby over one eye, cigarette on lip, smoke wreathing, out-of-key voice like the creak of the door to the john from where another man enters the bar, unseen except by the camera, and therefore us. He has a bulge in his pocket—a .38 perhaps—we won't know till the lab fishes out the bullets later. He draws a bead, fires twice. Stetson drops. Marcel screams, drops. Blood spatters. The man disappears. The pianist collects his music, shuts the lid of the piano, slips out through the side door. We follow. We're in the street now. The streets lights are fuzzy with rain. The music swells to full orchestral, the camera pans, there's a man running down the street, round the corner . . .

. . . into the cinema. He shuffles past turned knees, straining necks. People mutter. He trips over the feet of a young woman, almost stumbles into her lap, apologises, sits. She's wearing her best felt hat with the feather, her new blouse. She often comes here on her own. She's in no hurry to get home to cut sandwiches for her five brothers. It's Pathé news now, high stepping soldiers, thick arrows across maps. People sit here all day, smoking, eating. Dying. The double seats at the back are for the courting couples, but she's never been in one. She casts a sideways glance. She doesn't know him but what the hell. She'd have gone off with the dustman for half a crown. She smiles at him. He has artist's fingers. Never mind the blood, this is black and white, after all.

The main feature starts over.

He Carries His Innocence About Him

                                          as though
he might one day drop it or leave it on a bus. I am
starring in an old movie mouthing before a rolling screen
wound desperately on by a panting stage hand;
everything is no more than it seems and the script is
constantly rewritten. The actors duck behind the parapet
as the flying custards find the face of the walk-on
who was only looking for the coffee. Extruding critics
claim the whole affair would have been better left
or done on radio with a cast of thousands. I clench my teeth,
shape my fingers behind the light—look, a rabbit,
no, it's a cow. It's easy to create significance
in the drop of a handkerchief, a wave from a passing train.

Benevolent Advice

'Above all, never listen to Benevolent Advice' (The Prince)

The risk is, you will—take it, even,
never mind their smiles.
I get up early to read your words.
A ticking clock, a brewing bag—
proverbial. Your way of speaking
is fundamental, necessary.

The radio blurts out the downfall of a leader.

'Trim your enemy's strength
against himself.' He'll fall or win.
His name is an internal complaint
scribbled hurriedly on notes
with a query, before tests are ordered.

The Psychopathology of Everyday Life,
The Art of War.
'Too much reading at an early age
curdles the heart.' Do it.

'They doesn't deserve us
but they mean well.'
Does that count?

The Art of Politics

It's nearly six and we've ten miles to go
before we meet their mother, or whoever it is
she's sent to collect them this time.
The roads are dark and unfamiliar
and I'm driving too fast for a grandmother.
How can you judge time over 200 miles
when half the army and three police cars
take up two lanes for fifty minutes?
The solid November sun beats on my face
all the way to Leicester Forest.
Three KFCs and a banana.
They drop cardboard and fruit skins across the car seats.
They ask me what is a Conservative.
I say someone who eats babies.

The Naughtiest Girl in the School

Among the junkshop's cheap glasses, saltcellars,
plaster Alsatian (life-size), bronze cranes,
in a seaside town on the Firth of Forth
an hour's drive from the city—
a break after the jollies to clear our heads—
is a shelf of shabby books: a bible, *Endymion,*
and the Blyton I'd loved aged nine. 5 pence.

I know he'd have been just that, Dan,
this friend of yours, this thin lively man,
his research brief centred round street boys
and users. Last night at your graduation dinner
we talked about our childhood favourites—
his sly grin when I mentioned this title.

Call it coincidence. I buy it, slip it
into your hand: 'Give it to Dan, with love.'
A week later, a card of Chinese poppies,
and in his child-like writing 'thank you
for a remarkable evening'.

The Fishmonger's Daughter

Whelks, octopus, mackerel, cod.
No one's going to buy this lot.
A fish is a fish, and there's me schooled
in it, brought up to the trade.
Now I'm stuck with the leaky taps,
in a plastic apron and Dad's old cap.

Trawlermen, shag-tired and stinking,
haul their night's catch up the shingle
where fishwives fillet, slice and pack.
The men just want a beer and a crap,
to drop their tarps on some tart's vinyl
and sleep it off till the next nightfall.

When Dad got sick he made me promise
not to sell his precious business,
his clutching hands reeking carbolic.
eyes wide and damp like his best haddock,
Then he ups and offs to his bit in London
leaves me swinging in the wind.

When the sea's empty and quotas drop
I guess there'll be no more fish suppers
and I'll throw away my cap and apron,
scrub off the herring scales, find a man
whose face smells of cologne and lavender,
whose only ocean is off Bermuda.

But till he shows up with his wad and his yacht
I'll give the trawlermen all I've got.

Product Placement

His wife going off or the boss's final warning,
who knows, but that Tuesday Kevin
loaded the forklift with three cases of Hartley's,
five of Branston and six of Bells, tore
through the plastic flaps, down the Pampers aisle,
past the ready meals and the Kellogg's on special,
swerved round the checkout panicking Dawn
on her first day, crashed through the plate glass,
skirted two buggies and old Tom on his Shoprider,
straight under a BP tanker causing
a rush hour tailback halfway to Halifax.

Cath

The empty chemist's bottle on the shelf
reminded Cath that there was none so daft as
her. She'd have to fetch the pills herself,
with Debbie's show that night, and Kev on afters.

Bumping elbows in the kitchenette—
she and her brother Rob, twelve years apart
since he'd gone off to camp out in that squat
and she'd remained behind, and lived there yet,

just three doors up, within a minute's call
at night, or when the district nurse was off.
Still, better than that bloody hospital.
She caught Rob bite his nail, that jerky cough:

'You're off then?' 'Yes, I fixed to see this mate, er,
in Almondbury.' 'Well, say goodbye to mum.'
'No. No, you do it, say I'll see her later.
Take care.' He pecked her cheek, patted her bum.

'You dopey sod. Have these, you're looking thin.'
She thrust the bag of apples which he took,
knowing he'd only drop them in the bin
at the bus stop, without a backward look.

Spinney

One big swing off the beech tree into the banking,
weals of nettles and brambles on bare legs;
blue sky half shells scattered under bushes,
contents flown or eaten by rats or the ginger tom.

In the yellow shorts my mother made me
I run down the path of pine needles under the trees,
across to the turnpike for sticklebacks
stitching their path round the clear pebbles.

Mossy stones slippy by badger sets where
I creep at dusk in June to watch them rummage,
next to the pool I dig clay from, fingers grey,
cracked, like the old woman's I'll grow into.

It's all chained off now, the trees sawn down.
In the village pub on a rare visit I drink
with the firemen and farmers whose games I played,
avoiding their gaze, hoping they won't remember.

Breakfast

Dad has first read of *The Telegraph*
and mum will have the crossword later
in front of the telly when he's at the pub.

She stands by the stove to eat her porridge,
watching the eggs. He claps his hands,
as he did in India, when he wants more coffee.

I say Jesus would have been a socialist.
Jack de Manio gives the wrong time.
I shout goodbye but they don't hear me.

The wood pigeons cut short in the elm trees.
If I don't run I'll miss the bus.
The June air is yeasty as bread.

Dancing Class

Each Thursday after school
we change shoes, slip into the hall.
Estelle in net and stilettos
plugs in the Dansette,
poises for the quickstep
as we fumble for partners.
His hand grasps mine,
slightly damp. The tune floods

and on the beat she taps it out,
makes us repeat and repeat,
hands on shoulders, small of back:
step   step   stepandturn.
Too slow, too quick.
He stands on my foot.

The night air bites my throat.
He walks me to my stop.

Last Dance

I'm taking one step forward, two back, trying to work out
what had made me—'A' stream, Latin and Greek,
and university a fixed mark on the horizon I was
steering my boat towards—fall in love with a brickie who'd left
school at fifteen and who on the night I dumped him downed
thirteen pints with whisky chasers and ended up in a skip,
who used to take me dancing, mumbled the Drifters in my ear,
the vibrations so strong after forty years they buzz down my spine
to parts my mother never talked about but I was only too
well aware of as we shuffled round the dance floor and he pressured me
not to forget who was taking me home, a place I escaped from
two years later, and from him too, though I sometimes wonder
when I read about his chain of executive housing estates
if I made the right decision.

Theatre

Horton General Hospital, Summer 1962

The anaesthetist snaps an ampoule, drops
glass on the tiles for us to sweep up.
The man's still now. The surgeon stands
like a butcher, arms crossed, reckoning

a tray of meat. His scalpel slices a red grin,
hands plunge into the warm hollow,
haul out ropes of gut, snip a twist of gristle,
stuff the lot back in like a cushion.

Appendectomies, hernias, once an amputation.
Thursdays is gynae: dusting and cleaning.
They let me in to watch if I want to.
At first I fainted but you get used to it.

We collect patients, wheel them back,
enter their names in a tall book.
I'm nineteen, on a holiday job. Evelyn
is strung up with grief over her murdered son,

whose story stains our breaks and dinner hour.
On Saturdays we scrub corridor walls
spattered from the tonsillectomies,
balloon the rubber gloves to test for holes.

Chalk Farm

Blaring elephants echo from the zoo.
Friday evenings as you cross the Square
I watch from the fourth floor, throw down
the key. We're squashed into the side room

while my flatmate makes it with a violinist
just back from Prague and its brief spring.
She can get us freebies for the RFH,
acoustics crisp as sheets on a line.

Cheap folk nights in cork-lined rooms,
or a stroll up to Heath Street for a curry
over Primrose Hill where MacNeice heard
the trees felled at the start of the war.

'Summer of love'—that was last year.
You can see St Paul's from here, clear as a bell.

Pica

This year the summer solstice
is colder than the winter's,
and being pregnant I'm glad of it,
pushing a toddler and bags of shopping
in a purple kaftan, no car or supermarket,
shops a mile away,
home past the park, up Nightingale Lane
where the birds never sing.
Blood sugar low, pressure high, I rest
ears pounding by a wall to skin a banana
and an aproned woman offers an arm;
we stroll across the tarmac, stop by my door
with its cracked glass roses, and I long to be inside,
child down for a nap and me, legs up on the sofa
to ease my ankles, scoffing chunks of bread
from the best baker in London, gnawing slices
of Tilsit cheese, Greek olives, dill pickles and anchovies,
topped up with a large tin of full cream condensed milk.

Anniversary

Tuscan bean soup, a glass of Soave.
The perfect lunch! We should have stopped there.
The Pasta Puttanesca was a mistake,
especially as she said it came from whores
and we thought she said 'horse'.
But unlike language food has no boundaries,

and we're in Yorkshire, the sun's not shining,
the window overlooks the abattoir.
We no longer bother to count the years.
The past's foreshortened, autumn looms.
We'll stuff our faces till lighting up time
and when we've had enough we'll stagger home.

Dawn, North London

Our purple bedspread, the colour
of my wedding dress, of the seventies,
is black in the half light. Ghost faces grin
from the wardrobe's walnut shine.
The fluff under the bed would stuff a cushion.
Next to me a man is snoring.

Giggling whispers from the other bedroom:
they'll be on to us any second,
astride our stomachs like jockeys.
Somewhere else trains are racing through canyons,
moose forage across ice-capped hillsides.
A spider floats over the bed looking for home.

Candling

She procured me candles from Holloway
where she worked in the chapel, the honey
of their slippery stalks better than shop bought.
Our friendship fresh, our children on wary terms.

After we moved she asked me back:
New Year, a party. We lit candles,
kissed by their conniving light,
a rare snowstorm bedding the streets.

They used to hold eggs to candles,
gauging the shadow inside, if it was live.
She died ten years later, a woman's thing.
I was told this by a friend.

Domestic

A list on the kitchen table:
what needs doing,
where the lasagne is,
and the spare key.

They're not used to it,
says the cat.

But it's only one night.
Just turn on the oven,
it's all in there,
she says, combing her hair.

They stare from the window
as she runs down the path.

Put it on low, she shouts
getting into the car,
but they can't hear.

Snapshot

I'm standing by the door
dark unblinded windows and you
on your new computer sorting photos.
Midnight and the internet's down again.
A close night in September
our children back from Greece tomorrow
still clutching their grief
and I hear my voice saying the same thing
I say every year or so,
a mistake, I can't help it
though I'm not crying this time and you're smiling
that smile which says you can't handle this,
so I go to bed thinking we all die alone,
not just thinking it, saying it
but I'm not sure you're listening

Fruit

In his string vest circa 1968, the year of revolution,
a man with a calculator is working out
the circumference of the earth.

I peel oranges; the knife cuts so easily
through the cellulite skin.
What goes around comes around:

icy water pumped from the ground.
the taste of blackberries, their juice
on my fingers, my mouth.

Me and Ashbery Riding Shotgun on the M6,

my *Selected* firm against the wrist,
I wind down the window, fire
at the enemy juggernaut:

'Long ago was the then beginning to seem like now
As now is but the setting out on a new but still
Undefined way.'

Unsupported by reason's enigma
the tires slowly come to a rubbery stop.

He rang me yesterday

from Inner Mongolia where
he's shooting steam trains in the wild
and he lost his waterproofs
at the Russian border, 17 below.

I imagine it as I always do: me waiting
for him to arrive from somewhere,
hauling his case off a train he nearly missed
full of tales and desperate for a drink.

I'll tell him the headlines, the gossip.
I've filed the bills, thrown out
the offers, the winning numbers.
Our first Christmas card arrived yesterday,

There are no tourist shops in the wild
so all he's bought are
three flashing battery pens
and a telly tubby jigsaw.

He'll have been gone a month,
his hair longer. He'll settle into the car,
switch on the radio. *What have I missed?*

Pipe

In China you can pick up all sorts. A lighter
that plays 'The East is Red' on a flick of the wheel.
Plaques from lintels of ripped-out houses—
phoenix and dragon in curled combat,
bringers of fortune and long life.

I found a pipe in Shanghai, curved like a narrow
hunting horn, once ivory, now stained brown,
carved with snakes and flowers, yin and yang, I Ching.
You could dream a week away in its detail.
The man who sold it rubbed his shoulder, pointed:

I understood the thing was made of bone
but its use was lost on me until I saw
Once Upon a Time in America, De Niro
lost to the world in a New York opium den,
my pipe in his mouth.

Deals

1|

Glowing they bring in handfuls wrapped in her coat,
dug up under birch, spotted snow on red.
They poke the coals, their finds chopped and dried,
curled like flowers in honey jars, ready
to swap with friends for tobacco, fares,
the chance to end up round the right fire.

2

Two clocks droop on the wall. He giggles.
Once he stuffed Smarties in handfuls,
now his gold T-shirt cost sixty quid,
his jacket is cashmere, cool. One o'clock he leaves
to catch his mate, drop a tab; rises at five to drive his van,
motorway lights exploding like star shells.

Patch

Skewbald, large-lipped, ugly
as sin, he trod straight ahead
unfazed by traffic, hauling
the wagon filled with kids and tat,
putting up with the well-meaning:
their apples and cameras.

When it was over
he was sold to friends
to be set on another road,
or let free in a paddock,

or given back to the trader,
for god knows what—
but the kids didn't know that.
All their lives he'd been there
tethered to the roadside,
pulling grass with large yellow teeth.

When he went
they got a television.

Cousin Adelaide

In the wrong glasses she thumbs the album
clasped like a bible. Her focus blurred,
the generations slip, take strange identities—
I can't grasp who's dead, who's locked away.
Words tap out: Freda who stole the will.
Her mother. Six clocks syncopate.

On a stool by my knee the kettle boils.
Ulf, her Swedish help, who cooks her meals
and bandages her feet, hands round tea
and German raspberry cake from Shoreditch market.
Nowhere to put my plate. He stokes the fire.
The walls flake plaster on the two pianos,

the china dolls embracing in the corner,
her next OU assignment on Vermeer.
A cat leaps on my lap. She peers outside:
she thinks it's foggy, but it's a blizzard,
I have to go. I push past trunks, a bedstead,
the doll's house in the hall looped by geraniums.

I hug her on the step. She grabs my elbow.
From here they'd heard the IRA bomb Docklands.
She thrusts her mother's diaries into my bag.

.

Ringing Margaret

She doesn't answer.

The Central Middlesex remember her from last time
and refer me to the Robert Owen Psychiatric Day Centre
where the cleaner answers owing to its being Sports Day.

The number of the London Borough of Brent Social Services,
written last time on the back of an envelope, now belongs
to London Statistical Surveys. And either Brent, in an attempt
to abort the rebirth of capitalism, have refused to register
their new number, or Directory Enquiries are having an off day.

Her doctor's receptionist tells me
that the psychiatric social worker told them
that the downstairs lodger told him
that she was seen on Monday
so they weren't really worried.

She still doesn't answer.

On a folded piece of paper under the bookcase
is a list of useful numbers including
that of Brent Social Services, Area 6: May Frati.
May isn't in yet, but they find the file:
admitted Central Middlesex from Hammersmith, Tuesday.

Hammersmith?

Central Middlesex now confess
to having her in their possession,
not sectioned, merely for assessment.
I contact Brunel University Conference Centre hoping
Michael will get the message before he leaves
and he rings back at five to six because his watch is fast
and runs out of money too soon for explanations.

Swiss Pass

'Yes yes yes yes . . .' Ron our guide
agrees with everyone as usual.
He's been to this country thirteen times.
What he doesn't know he'll make up.

We can afford all this.
Specs and meds always at hand,
memories stretch way back.
We pose in our Dannimacs,

say the same things, reassuring,
stick to the way things are done.
Our maps are creased into fuzzy holes.

I've learnt the population of Switzerland,
its chief cantons,
its annual wine production in litres.

Caught 8.20 Brig to Montreux,
then the Golden Pass to Interlaken.
Snow on the Rothorn. Bought watch.

A man could lie buried here
for a thousand years.

Nose tilted under bifocals,
finger darting across columns,
Ron traces the minutiae of trains
to other ranges, better views,

provided it's clear: that's the only danger.

Maggie

Purple polyester tight on her thighs
she rushes out to meet us as we drive up.
She wants to tell us my father's OK,
she did his bit of shopping before we came,
keeps an eye out every morning.
She's breathless, cheeks the colour of her trousers.
'I still miss your poor mother.'
My father, on two sticks now, stays in his chair,
hating fuss. We leave at tea time, a long drive,
catch Maggie at her window, glass in hand,
bottle in the cupboard she keeps going back to.

Smoke

Salad and onions from the garden
lie in the colander waiting to be rinsed.
A radio play's drowned by our voices
and the boiling kettle. We're limp as the lettuce.
Your last weekend before you fly
to the States for ever, and though I'll visit
—trips to New York, New England in the fall—
we'll never again sit in my kitchen
over mugs of tea, giggling at Tarot cards,
oiling steaks for the barbecue. You fetch glasses.
I chop onions, poke charcoal till it catches.

On Not Being Able to Drive

In war, laden vans
drag along rough roads,
I was trapped,
unable to flee from the invader.

Learning was hard, expensive.
Fog and dark
turned roads where they shouldn't,
signs vanished.

Now filtered through red
I drive alone,
windows open on a draught
seemly and adequate as bread,

my car a frame, a locality
arbitrated for, confirmed,
from which I see waiting
the accessible mountains.

Summer Exhibition

#1.   Peach through to crimson, the Masquerade
are ending their first flush.

My artist neighbour fitting a window
smiles and waves, but his wife
tells me his ulcer's playing up:
the hanging committee's turned him down.

#2.   Their cool hall, a glimpse of the interior
and her by the mirror knotting a kerchief.

His gesso boards line the bare studio,
defined by beauty, true to themselves;
but he's a Calvinist: elect,
 justified by faith not works.

#3.   Washing the new window, arms lifted, breasts
rounded under the tightened blouse, she's
poised, squinting at the reflected sun,
always not quite wetting the glass.

Brighton Beach, 1960

Empty deck chairs line up in the blank light.
Beyond the pebbles the sea is out of sight.
The air is stiff with frying fish and seaweed.
People stare from the railings by the road.
Council flats loom over the aquarium.
The church is a long way off. Everyone likes the sun,
grit in their sandwiches and silly hats.
Soon they'll pack up, umbrellas will shut like traps
on a time when things were clearer cut, when men
were men and women kept their tops on.

Forest

Dave's shot a squirrel.
The landlord, who thinks he's a chef,
smokes and cooks it.
The .22 bullet's still above the bar.
Bacon hooks hang from the charred ceiling.
The Freeminer's tasty to visiting throats,
but true locals drink lager.

We chew thoughtfully.
Pam's young grandson sleeps against the wall.
The other side, they say, was Cromwell's
field hospital, filled with rubble now—a pity:
they could do with more space for barrels.
The talk's of a likely pardon for WW1 deserters.
Brian, a week's stubble, sunken eyes, downs his fourth—
he's off overnight to do some dodgy welding.

After a full English it's hot by the river.
The swans are stumbling on the shallow bottom.
A lack of grace. Neat swifts curve
into the paths of midges.
Long memories and nothing down on paper.
We've sat here an hour, a century,
under the oaks King Charles planted
to build the ships of the future,
not recognising the potential of iron.

Pietà

(along the road past Enna)

dry terraces
mountains beyond
the city built on a hilltop
sends messages to herdsmen
across gulleys and olive groves

dried gulleys slicing
the face of the mountains

rocks of thunder
cannon round the bus

heart dry
she holds her son
a long way off
a lightning charge
between them.

sun sets into a white sky
behind the crags
she clings to
like a charm

Rain

The books, the chair—it's as if he were breathing
down our necks as we break up the morning workshop,
listen on trannies to the music: Tallis, Bach,
friends' contributions, some of the poems.
And naturally wind and sun will compete across the hillside,
and it'll rain and we don't have the light on
so it's not surprising there's a shadow in the corner,
and when we hear the local vowels, his voice resounding
round the Abbey: 'Fear no more the heat o' the sun'
we know the thunder's answering and won't die down.

Picking Elderflowers

                    in June, I think of Rosa
dying. Insects settle on the blossoms
whose astringency battles
with pig farm and bonfires.

Later I strip them from their green stems,
or the wine will be bitter.
Carefully I extract the juices, avoid
letting in rogue yeasts.

After the funeral it's time
to strain the liquid into clean jars
to work slowly alone.
It will be ready in another year.

Gina's Story

i.m. Michelle

There's so much more I could tell you.
How can you judge the measure of a life?
Whose story is it, anyway? She lived,
she died. Often we thought we'd lost her,
each time I wrenched her back

with good nursing and unbiddable hope,
meanwhile rediscovering
some part of myself, the secret knowledge
in our genes. Her undernourished body,
her pretty hair, her cough: the images I carry.

He did more for her than any man could,
held the car door, warmed her coat by the fire.
Their wedding was the happiest day of my life.
At fourteen she'd still played with dolls.
All she'd ever wanted was a baby.

Nine weeks on oxygen, her drugs withheld.
One day a machine ground in her head.
They got him for rape, a little girl.
The lawyers used his suffering in mitigation:
'Dying wife saves local man from prison'.

We've got the boy now. He sleeps in her old room.
But she's been back. On his first birthday
we heard him laughing, someone calling his name.
Now when things go well I get afraid.
At times he has a look of her about him.

Canon

There's music that music buffs go for which
passes me by, like most of Shostakovich,
anything with trumpets, even Mozart when he's being tricksy.
Again, there's stuff which stops me short—so sexy,
fruitful, I'll have to have it at my funeral,
like 'Ain't No Sunshine When She's Gone' and that thing by Pachelbel.

How to Do Nothing

Get a grip, grab hold of your chattering mind,
shove your chattering mind into the grip, ignore
the squeals, shut the grip in a cupboard,
lock it, swallow the key. Rid yourself

of the thought that it is a sin not to be busy.
It is not a sin not to be busy. Good.
Sit. Do not immediately get up again
to fetch a book or a CD or answer the phone.

The beds will make themselves eventually
and you have enough food till Wednesday.
Ignore the cobweb hanging from the curtain rail
and the six dirty mugs and glasses on the carpet.

It was a boring evening anyway and you're glad
they didn't stay past midnight. Forget them
especially the friend of your friend's boyfriend.
He can find your number if he wants to.

Stare out of the window but do not start
a mental checklist: (1) prune the buddleia.
If there are birds or clouds let them move on.
What they portend is not your concern.

Sleep and death are the soft options.
Do not be tempted. You can do better.

[64]